By Ashley Martin

CONTENTS

INTRODUCTION

Karate is an exciting sport, and a traditional martial art with a fascinating history. Karate can be used for self-defence but has many other benefits, such as improving health, physical fitness and boosting self-confidence. The word 'karate' is derived from two Japanese characters: kara, which means empty, and te, which means hand.

ELEMENTS OF KARATE

Karate training is broken down into three sections.

BASICS (KIHON)

These are the fundamental techniques which make up karate, including stances, punches, blocks and kicks. The kihon are presented in the 'karate techniques' section of this book.

FORMS (KATA)

Kata are traditional choreographed sequences of moves performed as if fighting a series of imaginary opponents. The kata contain the self-defence techniques of karate, although understanding them takes years of training.

SPARRING (KUMITE)

The kumite section of karate involves sparring with a partner. At the beginner level, this is simply a set routine of punches and blocks. Some of these are covered in the 'Skills and Drills' section of this book. At the highest level, kumite is an unstructured fighting contest.

ORIGINS OF KARATE

Karate originated in Okinawa, a small island found near China, which is part of modern Japan. The traditional elements of karate were developed in Okinawa but have a strong Chinese influence. Modern elements of karate, such as sports karate and the belt system, originated in Japan.

EQUIPMENT

Karate does not require a lot of equipment. It has a simple, standardised uniform, and a variety of belt colours which signify the expertise of the individual. Aside from the uniform, the other equipment needed is designed to ensure safety.

KARATE UNIFORM

The karate uniform is called a *dogi*, or more often just *gi*, in Japanese.
Traditionally this is made from white cotton without much decoration, other than a club or association badge on the left breast. The gi is held together with a belt. The colour of the belt signifies rank.

PUNCH BAGS

Punch bags and strike shields are used to practise powerful kicks and punches.
For best results, attack as if your target is actually a few centimetres behind the bag, so that you put all your power into the target. Start slowly at first, then slowly increase the power.

FOCUS PADS

Use focus pads to improve your targeting and attacking speed.
Practise hitting the target in the centre. Some focus pads have target spots in the centre for you to aim at.

CRASH MATS

It is usual to practise karate moves without any mats, because the idea in karate is to stay on your feet.
However mats are often used in competition, so that you don't get hurt if someone sweeps or throws you. You should therefore use mats if you are doing any exercises which involve throws or sweeps.

The development of the karate student from beginner to expert is tracked using the coloured belt system.

The grades of the first ten belts are called kyu, and there are ten grades of black belt, called dan. Each belt requires you to demonstrate specific skills in a grading examination. If you train hard enough, you will usually be able to take an examination every three months. With regular training, most people are able to earn their black within three to five years.

White	**Orange**	**Red**	**Yellow**	**Green**	**Purple**
Beginner	*9th kyu – 3 months*	*8th kyu – 6 months*	*7th kyu – 9 months*	*6th kyu – 1 year*	*5th kyu – 1 year & 3 months*

Purple and White	**Brown**	**Brown and White**	**Brown and 2 White Stripes**	**Black**
4th kyu – 1 year & 6 months	*3rd kyu – 1 year & 9 months*	*2nd kyu – 2 years*	*1st kyu – 2 years & 3 months*	*1st dan – 3 years*

HOW TO TIE YOUR BELT

There are several correct ways of tying a karate belt.
A belt that has been properly tied is less likely to fall off during training. Tying your belt correctly takes only a little bit of practice.

Make sure you adjust the belt so that both of the ends look the same length at the end.

STEP 1

Pass the belt behind you and hold either end. Make sure that the belt is short on one side and long on the other.

STEP 2

Hold the short end closer to your middle and wrap the longer end around your body once. Then hold the two ends together near your navel.

STEP 3

Take the longer end that you wrapped around yourself, and tuck it under the double-thickness belt that you are holding by your navel.

STEP 4

Now tie a simple knot in the belt, and pull on both ends to tighten it.

PROTECTIVE EQUIPMENT

Protective equipment is rarely needed in a karate class. This is because any sparring exercises are expected to be performed with control, so that there is no danger of injury. However, for sparring matches or serious sparring training, some protective equipment is essential. Different competitions have different rules about what protection you must use, or are allowed to use.

HEAD GUARDS

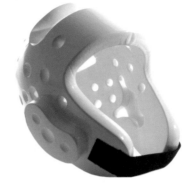

The standard head guard has padding for the sides of the head and the forehead. Some head guards also include a face grille. This is useful for protecting against the straight head punches which are so common in karate.

ARM PADS

Padding on the forearms can reduce the risk of bruising when blocking heavy attacks, or being blocked.

SHIN GUARDS

Padding on the shins protects against bruising in case of a leg clash when kicking, or when performing a foot sweep.

GROIN GUARDS

A groin guard is essential for any sparring match.

MITTS

Karate mitts cover the knuckles and the back of the hand. Some gloves also protect the wrist and part of the forearm.

CHEST PROTECTION

For most karate matches, men wear no chest protection. However women can wear a chest protector made of hard plastic, worn under the karate uniform. For full contact matches, both men and women wear a padded vest, which protects the front of the torso.

MOUTH GUARDS

A mouth guard (or gum shield) protects the teeth. If you are not wearing a head guard with a face grille, then a gum shield is essential for sparring. The best protection is offered by a professionally fitted gum shield, but many competitors opt for a 'boil and bite' self-fitted mouth guard.

FOOT GUARDS

Foot guards protect your feet when you are using kicking techniques during sparring matches.

THE KARATE DOJO

The karate dojo is the name given to any place where karate training takes place. Karate can be performed in almost any space, large or small. In good weather, it is even sometimes practised outside. However, karate classes almost always take place in a sports hall or custom-built dojo. When you enter the karate dojo, a certain level of behaviour is expected.

MENTAL PREPARATION

It is common to bow on entering and leaving the karate dojo.
This helps to prepare the mind for training and clear the mind before leaving.

PARTNER WORK

When participating in partner work, karate students must show respect to their fellow students at all times. They must show good control in all of their techniques, and keep the right distance from their partner so that no injuries occur.

THE INSTRUCTOR

Karate classes are taught by a karate instructor, who should also be a black belt. The intructor is called *sensei*, **which is a Japanese word for teacher.**
Pay attention to what your sensei tells you, and especially instructions regarding safety. If you are late for a session, wait for the instructor to indicate that you may start before joining in.

LINE WORK

Karate lessons normally start by lining up the students in belt grade order. Each grade then performs techniques appropriate to their level to the instructor's count.
Karate classes can range from six to 100 students in a lesson. To ensure that students can train safely, it is essential to line up the correct distance apart.

DOJO ETIQUETTE

There is a certain way that you will be expected to behave while in the dojo. You will have to follow specific rules:
- *Keep toenails and fingernails short.*
- *Do not wear jewellery or watches during training.*
- *Keep your training uniform clean and in good condition.*
- *Show respect to one another.*

THE COMPETITION AREA

While karate training can be done in any space, official competitions are held on a matted area, bordered by a safety area made up of different coloured mats. Usually the competition area is green and the safety area is red. If competitors do not stay within the competition area they are given a warning, or forfeit points to the opposition.

KEY INSTRUCTIONS DURING A FIGHT

The referee will give various instructions, often using Japanese terminology. These are the most important:

Hajime
Start. You must wait for the referee to say "hajime" before you start fighting.

Yame
Stop. You must stop fighting immediately.

Chui
Warning. If you break any rules, you will hear this as a warning.

Jogai
If you step out of the area the referee will shout 'jogai'.

THE COMPETITION SPACE

Judge's chair
The judges will assist the referee by using flags to indicate if they see any points being scored, or if anyone is breaking the rules.

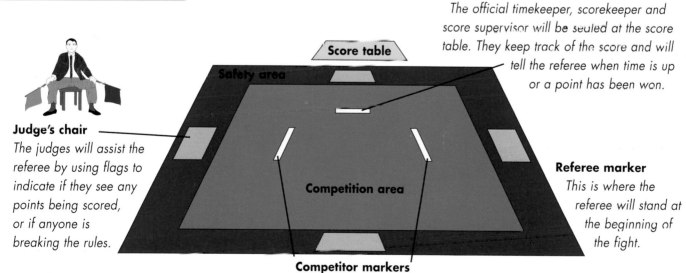

Score Table
The official timekeeper, scorekeeper and score supervisor will be seated at the score table. They keep track of the score and will tell the referee when time is up or a point has been won.

Referee marker
This is where the referee will stand at the beginning of the fight.

Competitor markers
There are two markers to indicate the starting positions of the competitors. Each time the fight is stopped, competitors must return to their markers.

Points Scoring
Points are awarded for different moves and the scorekeeper signals the number of points with arm gestures.

Ippon
1 point

Nihon
2 points

Sanbon
3 points

WARMING UP & STRETCHING

Most karate classes will start with a warm-up and stretching session, and will also often end with more stretches. Stretching is particularly important as it helps to improve your technique and performance in kicks. This is because it improves your flexibility.

KNEE BEND

Place your feet one shoulder-width apart.

Drop your weight by bending your knees, then lift up by straightening your legs.

KNEE LIFT

Stand with your feet one shoulder-width apart. Lift your knee, and try to raise it to the same height as your shoulder.

UPPER BODY ROTATION

Stand with your feet one shoulder-width apart. Put your arms up in front of you with your elbows bent.

Rotate slowly side to side. Let your feet twist as you turn, coming up on the ball of your rear foot.

STOMACH CRUNCH

Lie on your back with your knees bent and feet flat on the floor. Place your hands on your thighs and lift your upper body, so that your hands reach over your knees. Keep your lower body still.

ARM STRETCH

Reach across your body with your arm. Use your other arm to stretch it further by pushing above the elbow.

HAMSTRING STRETCH

Stand with your feet one shoulder-width apart. Keeping your legs straight, touch your toes.

QUAD STRETCH

Stand on one leg and lift your other leg behind you. Keep your back straight, and make sure your foot and knee are lifting straight back, not out to the side.

INSIDE LEG STRETCH

Place your feet two shoulder-widths apart. Keeping your legs straight, bend from the waist and reach to the floor.

Don't bounce when stretching. Moving slowly into a stretch works best.

STANCES

Stances are the foundation of karate technique. They are concerned with how you position your legs and body, but the way you position your hands will vary. Making the effort to improve your stances will not only make your karate look better – it will also help to build strong legs, which are the driving force behind strong, fast karate techniques.

FRONT STANCE – *ZENKUTSU DACHI*

Bend your front knee, putting most of your weight onto your front foot. Ensure that your front foot is pointing forward. Your rear foot should point forward at about 45 degrees.

Bend front knee

Rear foot at 45°

Front foot pointing forwards

45°

BACK STANCE – *KOKUTSU DACHI*

Bend your back leg, putting most of your weight onto your back foot. Ensure that your front foot points forward, and your back foot points out to the side. Your hips should be turned so that they face to the side.

Weight on back foot

Front foot pointing forwards

90°

HORSE-RIDING STANCE – *KIBA DACHI*

Bend both of your knees so that your weight is evenly distributed between either foot. Both feet should be pointing in the same direction.

Equal amount of weight on each leg

Feet parallel to each other

CAT STANCE – *NEKO ASHI DACHI*

Front leg slightly bent

Weight on back foot

Bend your back leg and put all of your weight onto your back foot. Bend your front leg slightly.

FIGHTING STANCE – *KAME*

Head faces forward

Hands up in guard position

Hips parallel to head

Front leg bent

Weight on toes

Put most of your weight onto your front foot, as you would in the front stance. Bend both knees and put more weight onto your toes than your heels. Keep your hands up in guard, protecting your body, but ready to punch forward. Your hips should be turned to the side, but your head should face forward.

PUNCHING

Punching is the most important technique in karate. Karate uses straight punches which travel directly from your hip to the target.

MAKING A FIST

You need to make a fist correctly so that you do not injure your hands when you punch. NEVER tuck your thumb inside your fingers.

STEP 1

Open your hand.

STEP 2

Curl in your fingers tightly.

STEP 3

Put your thumb on top of your fingers, tucking it in as much as possible.

STANDING PUNCH – CHOKU-ZUKI

Practise your punching while standing still, so that you can focus on good punching technique.

STEP 1

Start with your hands in fists, held by your hips.

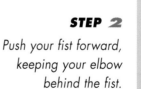

STEP 2

Push your fist forward, keeping your elbow behind the fist.

STEP 3

Straighten your arm and rotate your wrist. Make sure you keep your wrist straight.

STEPPING PUNCH – *OI-ZUKI*

The stepping punch is used when you need to close the distance between you and your opponent quickly.

45°

STEP 1 *Start in front stance.*

Slide foot forward

STEP 2

Slide your rear foot forward so that your feet come together. Start pulling the front hand back, while pushing the punching hand forward.

STEP 3

Keep your foot moving so that you finish in front stance as you complete the punch.

JABBING PUNCH – *KIZAMI-ZUKI*

The jabbing punch is a fast attack which can be aimed at the head level without compromising your defences. It can be used to test your opponent's defence, or to set up other, more powerful attacks.

Start in fighting posture and punch using the leading hand. Turn your hips so that your chest turns to the side, pushing your leading shoulder forward.

Push leading shoulder forward

Turn hips and shoulders

REVERSE PUNCH – *GYAKU-ZUKI*

The reverse punch is a stronger attack than the jab, but requires more commitment, and can expose you to a counterattack.

Start in the fighting posture and punch using the rear hand. Turn your hips so that your chest faces forwards, pushing your rear shoulder forward.

Push shoulder forward

Rotate hips

KICKING

Kicks are the most impressive aspect of karate, but they are also one of the most difficult aspects to master. Kicks require not only great skill and agility, but also strength and flexibility. When sparring, kicks have the disadvantage of being slower than punches and can result in a momentary loss of mobility. However, using your feet to attack leaves your hands free to defend – kicks are your most powerful attack.

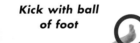

FRONT KICK – *MAE GERI*

Arms out to the side

The front kick is a very fast kick, and is usually performed with a snapping motion, hitting with the ball of the foot. Sometimes a thrusting motion is used to push the opponent back.

Raise knee

45°

STEP 1
Start in front stance with your arms straight out to the side. Keep your hands in this position throughout the kicking technique.

STEP 2
Lift your knee ready to kick. The higher you lift your knee the higher you can kick.

Kick with ball of foot

Hips move forward

Do not drop knee

Make sure that you have warmed up your leg muscles before trying any high kicks.

STEP 3
Extend your bent knee, kicking forward. Point the foot forward but pull your toes back, so that you make contact using the ball of your foot.

STEP 4
Immediately snap your foot back. Make sure you don't let the knee drop yet.

STEP 5
Land in front stance.

SIDE THRUSTING KICK – *YOKO KEKOMI*

Because it is a thrusting kick, this side kick can be used as a stopping or pushing kick. In self-defence situations, it can be used as a highly damaging attack to the side or back of an opponent's knee.

Knees are bent

Feet parallel

STEP 1
Start in horse-riding stance. Put your hands up as a fighting guard, pointing in the direction you are facing.

Step forward

Knees are bent

STEP 2
Step across one foot in front of the other. Make sure you keep your weight low and your knees bent.

Raise knee

STEP 3
Lift your knee ready to kick. If you lift your leg high, you will be able to kick high.

Heel higher than toes

Spin on back foot

STEP 4
Thrust your foot out. Turn your hips away from the kick, so that your foot turns sideways and your heel is slightly higher than your toes.

Spin on back foot

STEP 5
Pull your knee back, as in Step 3.

STEP 6
Step down into horse-riding stance.

SIDE RISING KICK – YOKO KEAGE

This side kick is similar to the side thrusting kick, but is much faster, using a more direct path and a fast push-pull hip action to whip the foot out and then back.

Side view

Knee points in direction of kick

Foot rests on knee

Feet parallel

STEP 1
Start in horse-riding stance.

Step forward

Knees are bent

STEP 2
Step across one foot in front of the other. Make sure you keep your weight low and your knees bent.

STEP 3
Lift the knee of your front leg, so that the foot you are going to kick with rests on your other knee. Point the kicking knee in the direction you are going to kick.

Hips move forward

Spin on back foot

STEP 4
Lift your knee higher and push your hips towards the target while straightening your leg.

Spin on back foot

STEP 5
Immediately snap the foot back to your knee.

STEP 6
Step down into horse riding stance.

ROUNDHOUSE KICK – *MAWASHI GERI*

The roundhouse kick (also known as the round or turning kick) is very popular in karate tournaments. Of all the kicks, it is the most likely to score points. Traditionally, it hits with the ball of the foot. However in tournaments, where it is necessary to make safe contact, it is usual to hit with the top surface of the foot.

Raise kicking foot almost as high as knee

Side view

STEP 1
Start in fighting stance.

45°

STEP 3
Rotate your hips.

Spin on foot

STEP 2
Lift your back leg. Angle your kicking leg so that your foot is almost as high as your knee.

Front view

STEP 4
Kick by letting your foot flick forward. Don't let your supporting foot stick to the ground or you won't be able to turn.

Spin on foot

STEP 5
Snap the foot back.

STEP 6
Step down into fighting stance.

TOP TIP
Improving flexibility is the key to improving your kicks. If you do 20 minutes of stretching each day you will quickly see improvements in how high you can kick.

BACK KICK – *USHIRO GERI*

This powerful kick hits with a thrusting action, using the heel.

STEP 1
Start in fighting stance.

Most of weight on front foot

Weight on toes

Rotate hips

Bring knee of back leg forwards and up

Supporting leg is slightly bent

Spin on foot

STEP 2
Rotate on the spot and lift your back foot. Bring your back leg forward and raise the foot close to the knee of your support leg.

Hips should turn down

Make contact using heel

Toes of kicking foot point towards ground

Supporting leg slightly bent

Supporting foot is able to move

Kicking foot returns to support knee

STEP 3
Thrust your foot backward in a straight line. Ensure that your kicking leg travels close to your support leg. As you kick, throw your arms in the direction of the kick.

STEP 4
Pull your foot straight back. Make sure that it moves in a straight line, and that your foot finishes on your knee.

HOOK KICK – URA MAWASHI GERI

The hook kick is also known as a reverse roundhouse kick. It is performed as if doing a thrust kick slightly off-target, but then hooking the leg in at the end to hit with your heel. In tournaments where it is necessary to make safe contact, it is usual to hit with the base of the foot.

Hands up in guard

Weight on toes

Lift front knee

Twist hips

STEP 1
Start in fighting stance, holding your hands up as a defensive guard.

STEP 2
Lift your front knee, keeping your hands in the guard position.

STEP 3
Twist your hip and kick, hooking your leg in to hit with your heel. To increase the power of the hooking action, you can bend your knee.

STEP 4
Pull your leg back, making sure that don't let your knee drop. Your leg should come back along the path that you used when kicking.

Don't let knee drop

STEP 5
Step back down into fighting posture.

BLOCKING

In karate, blocking techniques can be used to deflect incoming attacks and are key to defending yourself. These same techniques can be used as effective attacks when directed at an opponent. You can block with either hand, depending on where you expect an attack to come from.

DOWNWARD BLOCK – *GEDAN BARAI*

This block can be used to deflect low punches or kicks.

STEP 1
Prepare for the block by crossing your arms. Lift your blocking arm so that it is alongside your ear.

Blocking arm by ear

Leading arm straight

Weight on back foot

STEP 2
Step forward into a front stance and block down. Pull up the opposite fist to your hip. The blocking arm should twist at the end so that your palm faces down.

Swing blocking arm forward and down

Bring other hand back to hip

Rotate fist

Back leg is straight

Step forward with front leg

TOP TIP
USE THIS CHECKLIST TO IMPROVE YOUR DOWNWARD BLOCK:
• The fist of your blocking hand should finish just above your front knee.
• Your blocking arm should finish straight.
• Make sure your opposite fist is pulled back to your hip.
• Your body should be turned to the side so that you are hiding behind your blocking arm.

RISING BLOCK – AGE UKE

This block can be used to deflect head-level punches.

Non-blocking hand is open

Extend arm above head

Blocking hand pulls to hip

Legs are slightly bent.

Most of weight on back foot

STEP 1
Prepare for the block by pulling the blocking hand to your hip and reaching with the opposite hand.

Pull non-blocking arm back to support blocking arm

Move non-blocking arm forward and up

STEP 2
Start blocking as if punching up from the hip, and then vertically in front of your face. At the same time, pull back the opposite hand so that your arms cross.

Swing blocking hand up in front of forehead

Pull non-blocking hand back to hip

Most of weight on front foot

Back leg is straight

STEP 3
Step forward into a front stance and complete the block by pushing the elbow up. Pull the opposite fist to your hip.

TOP TIP
USE THIS CHECKLIST TO IMPROVE YOUR RISING BLOCK:
- The forearm of your blocking hand should finish just in front of your forehead.
- Your blocking arm should finish bent.
- Make sure your opposite fist is pulled back to your hip.
- Your body should be turned to the side so that your blocking arm is pushed forward.

OUTSIDE BLOCK – *SOTO UKE*

This is a powerful block that can be used to deflect stomach-level punches and thrusting kicks.

STEP 1

Prepare for the block by pulling the blocking hand behind your head, and reaching forward with the opposite hand.

Even if a technique requires body rotation, you should keep your head facing forward. Never take your eyes off your opponent.

Pull blocking arm back behind head

Blocking hand in fist

Reach straight forward with non-blocking hand

Weight on back foot

Bring blocking arm forward

Rotate body

Pull hand back to hip. Palm up

STEP 2

Step forward into a front stance and complete the block by rotating your body and swinging your blocking arm around. Pull the opposite hand to your hip. Rotate the blocking wrist so that your palm faces towards you.

Back leg straight

Most of weight on front foot

INSIDE BLOCK – *UCHI UKE*

This block is particularly useful for parrying roundhouse kicks or hooking punches.

Open non-blocking hand and reach forward

Blocking hand moves back

STEP 1
Prepare for the block by moving your blocking hand across your body and reaching with the opposite hand.

Standing on toes of front foot

Most of weight on back foot

Arm comes forward in smooth movement

Hand pulls back to hip

Back leg straight

Most of weight on front foot

STEP 2
Step forward into a front stance and complete the block. Pull back the opposite hand to your hip. Twist the blocking wrist so that your palm faces towards you.

TOP TIP
USE THIS CHECKLIST TO IMPROVE YOUR INSIDE AND OUTSIDE BLOCKS.
- The fist of your blocking hand should finish at the same height as your shoulder.
- Your blocking arm should finish bent 90 degrees.
- Make sure your opposite fist is pulled back to your hip.
- Your body should be turned to the side so that you are hiding behind your blocking arm.

KNIFE HAND BLOCK – *SHOTO UKE*

This block can be used to deflect stomach-level punches.

Both hands open

STEP 1
Prepare by opening both hands and crossing your arms, lifting your blocking arm so that it is alongside your ear.

Front leg straight

Palm faces outward

Leg bent

STEP 2
Step backwards into a back stance. Bring your blocking hand forward, with your elbow bent and your palm facing outwards. Pull the opposite hand back to the centre of your body.

Step back

Weight on back foot

TOP TIP
USE THIS CHECKLIST TO IMPROVE YOUR KNIFE HAND BLOCK.
• Hit with the fleshy part of the hand.
• Keep your fingers together.
• Keep your wrist straight.
• Don't let your elbows stick out. Keep them tucked in close to your centre line.

CROSS BLOCK – JUJI UKE

This block can be used to parry downward, swinging attacks.

Cross arms at wrists

Both hands open

Front heel raised

STEP 1
Prepare by opening both hands. Cross your arms at the wrists, in front of your stomach.

Usually when you block, you should turn your hips so that your body faces to the side. The exception is the cross block because it uses both hands to block.

Back leg bent

Weight on back foot

Hands move up together

Back leg straight

Weight moves to front foot

STEP 2
Step forward and thrust both hands out and up above your head.

TOP TIP
USE THIS CHECKLIST TO IMPROVE YOUR CROSS BLOCK.
- Keep your fingers together.
- Keep your wrists straight.
- Make sure you push the block high enough so any attack goes over your head.

FOOTWORK DRILLS

*G*ood footwork is key to winning karate sparring matches. If you are light on your feet and can move quickly, then you can more easily evade attacks, or hit your opponent when attacking. The key to fast footwork is to keep your weight on the balls of your feet and to keep your legs bent. This is hard work which requires strong muscles.

SLIDING JAB

This is a fast attack which can be used to test your opponent's defences, or as an opening move in a combination. It does not have the range of a stepping punch, but it is faster.

STEP 1

Start in fighting posture, with your weight on your front leg.

STEP 2

Slightly pick up your front foot and push with your back leg. This will propel you forward. Don't transfer weight to your back leg or you won't move as quickly. As you move forward, punch with your front hand.

Front foot slides forward

Arm bends

Back leg slides in

STEP 3

As your weight comes down on your front foot, drag your rear leg and punching arm in, so you finish in fighting stance ready for your next move.

SLIDING CROSS

This is not as fast as the sliding jab, but if done correctly it can penetrate your opponent's defences. The key is to use a strong hip motion to drive the punch forward.

Back leg straight

STEP 1

Start in fighting posture with your weight on your front leg.

STEP 2

As with the sliding jab, pick up your front foot slightly and push with your back leg. As you move forward, rotate your hips so your chest faces forwards, and punch with your rear hand to stomach level.

Rear hand punches

Drag rear leg in

Arm bends

STEP 3

As your weight comes down onto your front foot, drag your rear leg and punching arm in. You finish in fighting stance ready for your next move.

Use the switch to evade an attack and then immediately counterattack. This takes practice to get right. If you retreat too far, you will not be able to catch your opponent with the counterattack. If you do not retreat far enough, you might fail to evade the attack in the first place.

Weight on front leg

STEP 2

Slide your front leg back to meet your other leg while blocking down with your front hand. Try not to transfer too much weight to your back leg.

STEP 1

Start in fighting posture with your weight on your front leg.

STEP 3

Step forward with your other leg and punch to either head or stomach level.

If you use the correct footwork you can kick much faster. This footwork can be used with any of the kicks to produce a rapid kick attack. The key is to use your front leg to do the kick, and skip in quickly to close the distance.

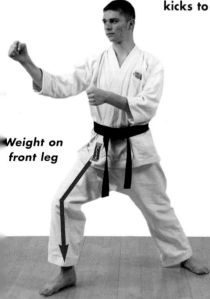

Weight on front leg

Rotate hips

Back leg slides back

STEP 1

Start in fighting posture.

STEP 2

Skip in with your back leg and immediately lift your front knee. Twist your hip to produce a roundhouse kick.

STEP 3

Slide your supporting leg back, and immediately bring your front foot down to take its place.

 TOP TIP
When using kicking attacks, make sure you keep your guard up. One of the advantages of using kicks is that your hands are free to defend you.

BASIC SPARRING DRILLS

*S*parring drills are used to practise attacking and defending with a partner. All karate techniques must be used with appropriate control, which means stopping your attacks just short of actually hitting your partner. This is especially important when performing a head-level attack.

DEFENCE AGAINST HEAD-LEVEL PUNCH

Defender

Opponent

Weight on front foot

Push blocking arm up

Rotate body

STEP 1

Face your opponent in fighting stance.

Slide back with both feet

STEP 2

As your opponent punches, slide back and deflect the punch above your head with a rising block. Twist your body so that your blocking arm is pushed forward toward the attack. Pull your opposite arm back in preparation for your counterattack.

Pull blocking arm back to hip

Reverse punch

Rotate hips

STEP 3

Punch with your non-blocking hand, rotating your body so that your arm is pushed forwards and can reach your opponent. This is called a reverse punch.

Defender   **Opponent**

DEFENCE AGAINST MIDDLE-LEVEL PUNCH

Weight on toes

STEP 1

Face your opponent in fighting stance.

Swing blocking arm in

Pull arm back

Twist body

Slide back

STEP 2

As your opponent punches, slide back and deflect the punch to the side with an outside block. Twist your body to add extra power to the block. Your opposite arm should be pulled back in preparation for your counterattack. At the end of the blocking motion your body should be turned to the side, so that it is hidden behind your blocking arm.

Pull blocking arm back to hip

Rotate hips

Punch to stomach

STEP 3

Rotate your body as you reverse punch, so that your punching arm is pushed forwards far enough to reach your opponent.

TOP TIP
Don't overreach by leaning so that your head comes forward when you punch. If you are too far away, then you need to use your legs to make up the distance.

DEFENCE AGAINST FRONT KICK

Defender

Opponent

Weight on front foot

STEP 1

Face your opponent in fighting stance.

Put most of your weight onto your front foot, as you would in the front stance. Bend both knees and put more weight onto your toes than your heels. Keep your hands up in guard, protecting your body, but ready to punch forward. Your hips should be turned to the side, but your head should face forward.

Block with front arm

Back foot slides to side

Blocking arm to hip

Rotate hips

Punch with non-blocking arm

Slide foot forward if necessary

STEP 2

As your opponent kicks, evade by sliding to the side and hitting the inside of the leg with a downward block. Don't try to parry the kick – you will not be able to safely stop such a strong attack with direct force. Instead, use your body motion as your main defence and aim for your block to contact with the side or underside of the kicking leg.

STEP 3

Reverse punch to the stomach. Remember to turn your hips in order to reach your opponent. If this is not enough, then you can slide forward to reach further.

DEFENCE AGAINST SIDE KICK

Defender

Opponent

Weight on toes, ready to move

STEP 1

Face your opponent in fighting stance.

Outside block to opponent's leg

Slide to the side

STEP 2

As your opponent kicks, evade by sliding to the side and hitting the back of the leg with an outside block. However, you should not try to reach the kick if it was very low or off target, as you will lose your posture.

Punch to stomach

Blocking hand to hip

STEP 3

Counterattack with a reverse punch to the stomach. If you made contact with your block then you may have pushed your opponent off-balance. In this case you will be able to counterattack with a reverse punch aimed at their back.

TOP TIP
When blocking a kick, you must use body motion to evade the kick. If you try to block head-on using brute force alone, you will risk bruising your arm.

DEFENCE AGAINST ROUNDHOUSE KICK

Defender

Opponent

Weight on front foot

STEP 1

Face your opponent in fighting stance.

Put most of your weight onto your front foot, as you would in the front stance. Bend both knees and put more weight onto your toes than your heels. Keep your hands up in guard, protecting your body, but ready to punch forward. Your hips should be turned to the side, but your head should face forward.

STEP 2

As your opponent kicks, evade by sliding away from the kick and ward off the leg with an inside block. Rotate your body and swing your blocking arm around. Make sure that you keep your blocking arm tense at the point of impact in order to stop this kick.

Keep blocking arm tense

Back foot slides to side

Swing body round

Reverse punch to stomach

Twist hips

Slide foot forward if necessary

STEP 3

As your opponent steps forward after the kick, counterattack with a reverse punch aimed at the stomach.

Defender

Opponent

Weight on toes, not heels

DEFENCE AGAINST BACK KICK

STEP 1

Face your opponent in fighting stance.

Put most of your weight onto your front foot, as you would in the front stance. Bend both knees and put more weight onto your toes than your heels. Keep your hands up in guard, protecting your body, but ready to punch forward. Your hips should be turned to the side, but your head should face forward.

Bring blocking arm forward to opponent's leg

Rotate body

STEP 2

This kick is very hard to stop, but quite easy to deflect. So, as your opponent kicks, evade by sliding to the side and deflecting the leg with an outside block. With practice, you will find that you will even be able to move in close to your opponent when performing this defence, as long as you move off the line of the attack.

Evade by sliding back foot sideways

Reverse punch to back or ribs

Rotate at hips

STEP 3

Your opponent will step forwad after the kick, and will find that they have moved past you. You are now to their side, in what is called a flanking position. Counterattack with a reverse punch to the back, or the ribs.

ADVANCED SPARRING DRILLS

Putting moves together in attacking combinations can really help you to score points in a sparring match. Practise these set pieces so that they are second nature. This will give you the best chance of using them successfully when you need them.

ROUNDHOUSE KICK COMBINATION

A good way to score with a roundhouse kick is to force your opponent to bring their hands up to protect their head. By doing this they will expose their body, and present a target for your roundhouse kick.

Opponent   Attacker

STEP 1

Face your opponent in fighting stance.

Jab with front hand

Slide foot

STEP 2

Move into attack range by sliding your front foot forward while throwing a jab to the head. This will draw your opponent's guard up.

Pull fist back to hip

Aim for head

Twist hips

STEP 3

Push your opposite hip forward and throw a reverse punch to the head, again forcing your opponent to block.

Kick to back

Twist hips

Twist on foot

STEP 4

Continue the forward motion of your hip. Lift your right knee and perform a roundhouse kick to the body, which will be unprotected.

FOOT SWEEP COMBINATION

A foot sweep is a great way to unbalance your opponent so that you can easily score a point, but a sweep won't work if your opponent's weight is on the front foot. This combination uses head attacks to make your opponent move backwards, taking weight off the front foot and making them open to a foot sweep.

Opponent   **Attacker**

Twist your body

Slide foot

STEP 1

Start in a fighting stance. Slide your front foot forwards and jab to the head. You can improve your reach by twisting your body to the side, so that your punching arm is pushed forwards.

Punch to the head

Twist at hips

Weight moves to back foot

STEP 2

Twist your body in the opposite direction, and reverse punch to the head. Your opponent's weight will move onto their back leg. It is important that this punch is aimed at the head, so as to unbalance them.

Opponent is knocked off balance

Hips continue to rotate

Swing back foot behind opponent's foot

STEP 3

Continue the forward motion of your hip. Swing your back leg round using it to sweep your opponent's front foot.

Reverse punch

Hand back to hip

Twist feet

Move weight to front foot

STEP 4

You could use a sweep, but a sweep is not considered a finishing move. If you succeed in unbalancing your opponent, then follow up with a reverse punch.

SELF-DEFENCE

Karate is an effective form of self-defence. When practising self-defence techniques with your partner, take special care not to injure them.

ESCAPE FROM A WRIST GRAB

Opponent   Defender

Opponent grabs wrist

STEP 1

This move can be used when your opponent tries to grab your wrist.

STEP 2

Step out to the side and swing your arm out the same way. Make sure that you turn your whole body to the side and bend your front leg.

Twist shoulders and hips

Bring arm across body

Twist foot 90 degrees

Take hold of wrist and elbow

Push arm forward

Rotate hips

STEP 3

Keep your hand moving in a big circle. Your other hand should join in this movement, pushing on your opponent's elbow. Use your whole body to drive this movement, by rotating your hips.

Put weight on elbow

STEP 4

Circle your hand down, grasping their wrist and pressing down with your other hand on the elbow. Put your body weight behind this movement by bending your front knee and dropping your weight down.

Opponent

Defender

Opponent uses bear hug

STEP 1

Use this move if your opponent grabs you from behind.

Rock head back

STEP 2

Rock backwards pushing your head into your opponent's face. This will act as a distraction and may weaken their hold on you.

Strike stomach with elbow

Step side-ways

STEP 3

Rock forward again and step out to the side, bending your knee so that you drop your weight. At the same time, swing your arm back, elbowing your opponent in the stomach.

Take hold of their arm

STEP 4

Grab your opponent's arm with both hands.

Hold on tight and turn your body

Drop weight to opposite foot

STEP 5

Hold your opponent's arm tightly. Partly lift your opponent, as if you are lifting a heavy backpack onto your shoulder. Turn your body and drop your weight onto the opposite foot, throwing your opponent.

DEFENCE AGAINST DOWN SWING

An aggressor could be attacking with a weapon, and if this is the case it is important to block this attack on their arm, trying not to make contact with the weapon.

Defender   *Opponent*

STEP 1

Your opponent raises their hand and prepares to attack.

Raise arms to block

STEP 2

Block the downward motion by crossing your arms, and warding off your opponent's forearm.

Step forward with front foot

Grab wrist   **Push down on their elbow**

STEP 3

Grab your opponent's wrist with your right hand, while pressing on their elbow with your left hand. Step past your opponent and lock their arm straight by applying pressure to the elbow.

Step forward   **Continue to apply pressure**

STEP 4

Step in towards your opponent's elbow, keeping it locked straight. Bend your front knee, dropping your weight down on their arm to bring them to the ground, allowing you to restrain them or to escape.

DEFENCE AGAINST HOOKING PUNCH

Opponent
Strike with palm
Defender
Block

A swinging punch is a common attack by untrained fighters. It is a powerful attack, but is easy to defend against.

STEP 1

Your opponent swings a hooking punch. Ward off the punch with an inside block, and at the same time counter by striking with your palm to the attacker's chin.

STEP 2

Step forward, hooking your foot in behind your opponent's front leg, so that you finish close in to them. Push under their chin so that they lean back.

Push under chin

Hook your foot behind opponent's leg

Grab and pull wrist

Step back with front leg

Do not attempt throwing techniques unless your partner knows how to fall safely. Use soft crash mats to help break the fall.

STEP 3

Grab your opponent's wrist with your right hand. Thrust your front leg back, so that it trips your opponent by lifting their front leg. At the same time, push down on your opponent's upper body with your right hand, and pull their wrist with your left hand.

KARATE TOURNAMENTS

The World Karate Federation (WKF) is the recognised International Sport Federation for karate and represents the general consensus of the rules from the various styles of karate.

There are four main types of karate events:

- Individual kata
- Team kata
- Individual kumite (sparring)
- Team kumite (sparring)
- Kumite rules (sparring)

SCORING POINTS

In a *kumite* match, the competitors can score points using effective, but controlled, techniques. Successful attacks score one, two, or three points depending on how difficult they are to perform. The match finishes when either competitor has scored eight or more points, or the time limit for the match is reached.

Attacks are limited to the following areas:

- Head
- Face
- Neck
- Abdomen
- Chest
- Back
- Side

3 POINTS – *SANBON*

The most difficult attacks score three points – or *sanbon* in Japanese.

Punches on ground:
This involves throwing or leg-sweeping the opponent to the mat, then following this with a scoring technique like a punch.

Head-level kicks:
The round-house kick is the most commonly used head level kick in karate matches.

Punches on the back:
These include punches to the back of the head and neck.

These intermediate moves score two points, which translates to Japanese as *nihon*.

Stomach-level kicks:
Front kicks and side thrusting kicks can be used, but the roundhouse kick is the most commonly used kick in karate matches.

Combination hand techniques:
An example of this would be a jabbing punch to the head, followed by a reverse punch to the body.

Sweeps:
Unbalancing the opponent, for example with a foot sweep, and scoring, for example with a reverse punch.

The quickest and easiest attacks score only one point, which is *ippon* in Japanese.

Punches:
For example, a jabbing punch to the head.

Backfist strikes.:
This attack involves snapping the arm forward from the elbow, to strike with the back of the fist.

These techniques are considered too dangerous to use in a karate tournament.

- **Knee strikes**
- **Elbow strikes**
- **Head butts**
- **Open handed techniques to the face**
- **Any attack which makes contact with the throat**

DIET & MENTAL ATTITUDE

*E*ating healthily for both karate training and karate competitions can give you the edge. It can improve your performance by making sure that you have plenty of energy for physical activity.

DIET

This is the recommended intake for a balanced and healthy diet, which is essential for karate experts.

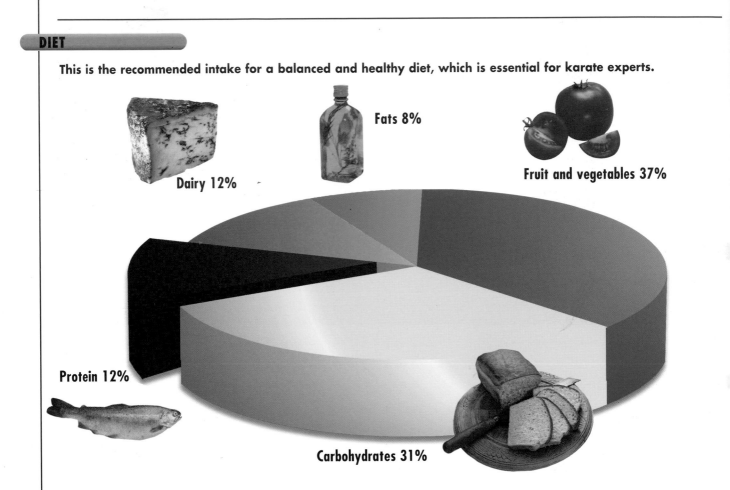

Dairy 12%

Fats 8%

Fruit and vegetables 37%

Protein 12%

Carbohydrates 31%

BEFORE TRAINING

Before training, you should eat carbohydrates, which are good energy foods.

Karate training sessions normally last between one and two hours. Snacks eaten within an hour before exercise should keep you from feeling hungry. Karate competitions, on the other hand, tend to be all-day events with many breaks. So it's best to keep carbohydrate snacks such as bananas and sandwiches close at hand.

DURING TRAINING

Karate can be hot work, so it's important to stay hydrated.

It is a good idea to hydrate before beginning any exercise, and then to re-hydrate regularly after the first 30 minutes of exercise. Water is suitable for short training sessions. Sports drinks that contain sugars are more effective for longer training sessions.

MENTAL ATTITUDE

Physical training is only part of karate. An essential component is your mental attitude. Training to become a black belt, and training for competitions requires patience and dedication. Karate performances can be determined by how confident you look.

AWARENESS

You should be aware of your surroundings and your opponent. The Japanese call this zanshin. You need to be aware of an imminent attack in order react to it and to defend yourself.

OPEN MIND

Being aware of an imminent attack is not enough. You must also be in the correct state of mind in order to react to that attack. This means that you need to have an open mind, which is able to react to any attack. The Japanese call this mushin. If you build a plan around only one particular attack, then you will be unable to act quickly if that expectation is wrong. Fear is a barrier to an open, reactive mind. Through karate training you will be able to overcome the fear of being hit, and this will enable you to react quickly.

STRONG SPIRIT

A strong spirit and positive mental attitude will enable you to overcome setbacks and challenges. One method used by karate practitioners to build spirit is to use a martial shout called a kiai. Using a strong kiai when you attack will build your courage and spirit, while working to intimidate your opponent.

PERSEVERANCE

Training to become a black belt can take anywhere between three and five years. A typical student will train two to three times a week for this duration of time. Therefore, to become a proficient martial artist takes many years of training and commitment. Staying motivated and on track to achieve this goal is essential. Karate training is mostly about repeating moves until they start to become natural reactions.

COURTESY AND RESPECT

You should be polite to everyone and that includes your opponents. If you do not have respect for your opponent's abilities, then you are in danger of underestimating them.

DON'T PANIC!

Stay calm and focused. Never lose your temper: karate requires that you use focused aggression, not anger. People who get angry act foolishly and without forward thinking, and are easily defeated.

HOW THE EXPERTS DO IT

Karate tournaments are very popular among young people participating in karate. They are particularly popular with university students.

MONEY

There is little money to be made from winning karate tournaments, and most competitions offer no prize money at all.

Winners of big karate tournaments can build their fame, and use this to further other careers. For example, movie stars like Cynthia Rothrock and Jean-Claude Van Damme were successful karate competitors before they starred in martial arts movies. However, most people who go on to become professional karate practitioners do so by running their own clubs or karate associations.

Japanese karate champion Yuka Sato poses with a bouquet and mascot at the Olympics.

Wayne Otto (OBE) is the most successful British karate competitor of all time. He's the holder of nine World Championship titles.

COMPETITIONS

There are many different types of karate competitions.

The smallest are internal club competitions which only take one or two hours. The largest are international tournaments like the Shoto World Cup, which takes three days. In between, there are various regional and national tournaments which usually take one day.

A typical tournament day might look like this:

7.00   *Wake up*
7.30   *Eat high energy breakfast*
8.00   *Get on team bus and travel to venue*
9.15   *Arrive at venue and register*
9.30   *Get changed*
9.45   *Team warm-up and pep talk*
10.00 *Tournament starts. Competitors wait for their events in preliminary rounds.*
16.00 *Final rounds*
17.00 *Medals award ceremony*
18.00 *Tournament finishes. Return to bus and head home.*
19.30 *Team dinner. Reflect together on successes and failures of the day.*

The actual bouts that you are involved in may only last one or two minutes each, which will mean a lot of sitting around and waiting.
During this time, make sure you stay warm and have snacks on hand to keep energised. It can be useful to watch other competitors to analyse their strengths and weaknesses because you might meet them in later rounds.

Two karate experts face off in a championship match.

GLOSSARY

COUNTER – An attack used in response to or to block an opponent's attack.

CRASH MAT – A thick pad placed on the floor to protect someone falling on the ground.

DAN – The level of achievement of someone who has reached black belt.

DOJO – Karate training hall. This literally means 'place of the way'.

EVADE – To dodge an attack.

FIGHTING STANCE – An informal fighting stance with the arms ready to attack or defend and the legs bent to allow for rapid movement.

FOCUS PAD – A small pad for practising the accuracy of strikes.

FRONT STANCE – A formal posture often used for lunge attacks with most of the weight on the front knee.

GI – Name given to the traditional karate uniform. It is usually white cotton held together with a coloured belt.

HAMSTRING – A tendon in the back of the knee.

JAB – A fast punch using the leading hand.

KATA – Traditional forms usually consisting of between 20 and 110 choreographed moves, as if fighting a series of imaginary opponents.

KYU – A grade below black belt. The highest of these grades is 1st kyu and the lowest is usually 10th kyu (white belt).

PARRY – Defending against an attacking move.

QUAD – This is short for quadricep, a muscle on the front of the thigh.

SENSEI – Karate instructor.

SPAR – To fight in a stylised way, without putting your full strength into attacks.

SWEEP – A leg technique intended to knock an opponent's foot or lower leg in order to unbalance them.

THROW – A grappling move whereby an opponent is unbalanced and is forced to fall to the ground.

LISTINGS

World Karate Federation
Galería de Vallehermoso 4, 3rd floor,
28003 Madrid, Spain
Tel: 0034-91-535-9632 Fax: 0034-91-535-9633
Website: www.karateworld.org

English Karate Federation
23 Sidlows Road, Cove,
Farnborough, Hants, GU14 9JL
Tel: 0770 888 880
Website: www.englishkaratefederation.com

International Shotokan Karate Federation
222 South 45th Street,
Philadelphia, PA 19104, USA
Phone: 001-215-222-9382 Fax: 001-215-222-7813
Website: www.iskf.com

The International Traditional Karate Federation
930 Wilshire Blvd. Suite 1007,
Los Angeles, CA 90057, USA
Phone: 001-213-483-8262 Fax: 001-213-483-4060
Website: www.itkf.org